AMANDA GORMAN

THE HILL WE CLIMB

AN INAUGURAL POEM *FOR THE* COUNTRY

❧ FOREWORD BY **OPRAH WINFREY** ❧

VIKING

FOREWORD

by OPRAH WINFREY

THEY DON'T COME very often, these moments of incandescence where the welter of pain and suffering gives way to hope. Maybe even joy.

Where a deep distress that has dogged our souls and shaken our faith—so difficult to articulate and even harder to bear—is transformed into something clear and pure.

Where wisdom flows in cadences that sync with the thrum of our blood, the beat of our hearts.

Where grace and peace in human form take the measure, seeing where we've been and where we must go, lighting the way with her words.

She was exactly what we'd been waiting for, this "skinny Black girl, descended from slaves," showing us our true selves, our human heritage, our heart.

Everyone who watched came away enhanced with hope and marveling at seeing the best of who we are and can be through the eyes and essence of a twenty-two-year-old, our country's youngest presidential inaugural poet.

As her words washed over us, they healed our wounds and resurrected our spirits. A nation, "bruised but whole," climbed up off its knees.

And finally, a miracle: we felt the sun pierce the "never-ending shade."

That is the power of poetry. And that is the power we collectively witnessed at the inauguration of President Joseph R. Biden on January 20, 2021.

The day Amanda Gorman, profoundly presenting her fullest, most radiant self, rose to the microphone and the Moment . . . giving us the gift of "The Hill We Climb."

Read by the poet
at the inauguration of
President Joe Biden
January 20, 2021

THE HILL WE CLIMB

Mr. President and Dr. Biden,
Madam Vice President and Mr. Emhoff,
Americans, and the World:

When day comes, we ask ourselves:

Where can we find light

In this never-ending shade?

The loss we carry, a sea we must wade.

We've braved the belly of the beast.
We've learned that quiet isn't always peace,
And the norms and notions of what "just is"
                    Isn't always justice.

And yet the dawn is ours before we knew it.
                    Somehow, we do it.
Somehow, we've weathered and witnessed
A nation that isn't broken, but simply
  unfinished.

We, the successors of a country and a time
Where a skinny Black girl,
Descended from slaves and raised by a
  single mother,
Can dream of becoming president,
Only to find herself reciting for one.

And yes, we are far from polished,
    far from pristine.
But this doesn't mean we're striving to
    form a union that is perfect.
We are striving to forge our union with
    purpose,

To compose a country committed
To all cultures, colors, characters,
And conditions of man.
And so we lift our gazes not
To what stands between us,
But what stands before us.
We close the divide,
Because we know to put
Our future first, we must first
Put our differences aside.

We lay down our arms

So that we can reach our arms out to one
    another.

We seek harm to none, and harmony for all.

Let the globe, if nothing else, say this is true:

That even as we grieved, we grew,

That even as we hurt, we hoped,

That even as we tired, we tried.

That we'll forever be tied together.

   Victorious,

Not because we will never again know

   defeat,

But because we will never again sow

   division.

Scripture tells us to envision that:

"Everyone shall sit under their own vine
　　and fig tree,

And no one shall make them afraid."

If we're to live up to our own time, then
　　victory

Won't lie in the blade, but in all the bridges
　　we've made.

That is the promised glade,

The hill we climb, if only we dare it:

Because being American is more than a
　　pride we inherit—

It's the past we step into, and how we
　　repair it.

We've seen a force that would shatter our
    nation rather than share it,
Would destroy our country if it meant
    delaying democracy.
And this effort very nearly succeeded.
But while democracy can be periodically
    delayed,
It can never be permanently defeated.

In this truth, in this faith, we trust.

For while we have our eyes on the future,

History has its eyes on us.

This is the era of just redemption.

We feared it at its inception.

We did not feel prepared to be the heirs

Of such a terrifying hour.

But within it we've found the power

To author a new chapter,

To offer hope and laughter to ourselves.

So while once we asked: How could we
   possibly prevail over catastrophe?
Now we assert: How could catastrophe
   possibly prevail over us?

We will not march back to what was,
But move to what shall be:
A country that is bruised but whole,
Benevolent but bold,
Fierce and free.

We will not be turned around,

Or interrupted by intimidation,

Because we know our inaction and inertia

Will be the inheritance of the next
  generation.

Our blunders become their burdens.

But one thing is certain:

If we merge mercy with might, and might
  with right,

Then love becomes our legacy,

And change, our children's birthright.

So let us leave behind a country better
than the one we were left.
With every breath from our bronze-
pounded chests,
We will raise this wounded world into
a wondrous one.

We will rise from the gold-limned hills
   of the West!
We will rise from the windswept
   Northeast, where our forefathers first
   realized revolution!
We will rise from the lake-rimmed cities
   of the Midwestern states!
We will rise from the sunbaked South!

We will rebuild, reconcile, and recover,
In every known nook of our nation,
In every corner called our country,
Our people, diverse and dutiful.
We'll emerge, battered but beautiful.

When day comes, we step out of the
   shade,
Aflame and unafraid.
The new dawn blooms as we free it,
For there is always light,
If only we're brave enough to see it,
If only we're brave enough to be it.

AMANDA GORMAN

became the sixth and youngest poet, at age twenty-two, to deliver a poetry reading at a presidential inauguration. She is a committed activist who works on the local, national, and international levels to advocate for the environment, racial justice, and gender equality. Amanda's work has been featured on *The Today Show*, PBS Kids, and *CBS This Morning*, and in *The New York Times*, *Vogue*, *Essence*, and *O, The Oprah Magazine*. She is also the author of the forthcoming picture book *Change Sings*, illustrated by #1 *New York Times* bestselling illustrator Loren Long, as well as the poetry collection *The Hill We Climb and Other Poems*. After graduating from Harvard University, she now lives in Los Angeles. Please visit theamandagorman.com.

VIKING
An imprint of Penguin Random House LLC, New York

First published in the United States of America by Viking,
an imprint of Penguin Random House LLC, 2021

Visit us online at penguinrandomhouse.com.

LIBRARY OF CONGRESS CATALOGING-IN-PUBLICATION DATA IS AVAILABLE.

Printed in the United States of America

ISBN 9780593465271

1   3   5   7   9   10   8   6   4   2

Design by Jim Hoover   Text set in Dante MT Std